TREASURE HOUSE

Pupil Book 6

Spelling Skills

Authors: Sarah Snashall and Chris Whitney

William Collins' dream of knowledge for all began with the publication of his first book in 1819.

A self-educated mill worker, he not only enriched millions of lives, but also founded a flourishing publishing house. Today, staying true to this spirit, Collins books are packed with inspiration, innovation and practical expertise. They place you at the centre of a world of possibility and give you exactly what you need to explore it.

Collins. Freedom to teach.

Published by Collins
An imprint of HarperCollins*Publishers*
The News Building
1 London Bridge Street
London
SE1 9GF

Browse the complete Collins catalogue at
www.collins.co.uk

Publishing Director: Lee Newman
Publishing Manager: Helen Doran
Senior Editor: Hannah Dove
Project Manager: Emily Hooton
Authors: Sarah Snashall and Chris Whitney
Development Editor: Jessica Marshall
Copy-editor: Tanya Solomons
Proofreader: Tracy Thomas
Cover design and artwork: Amparo Barrera and Ken Vail Graphic Design
Internal design concept: Amparo Barrera
Typesetter: Jouve India Private Ltd
Illustrations: Leesh Li (Beehive Illustration) Beatriz Castro, Aptara and QBS
Production Controller: Rachel Weaver

Printed and bound by Grafica Veneta S.p.A.

Acknowledgements

The publishers wish to thank the following for permission to reproduce photographs. Every effort has been made to trace copyright holders and to obtain their permission for the use of copyright materials. The publishers will gladly receive any information enabling them to rectify any error or omission at the first opportunity.

p6 losw/Shutterstock, p18 Kar/Shutterstock, p30 Miyu Nur/Shutterstock, p32 Lorelyn Medina/Shutterstock, p36 dimnikus/Shutterstock, p49 kontur-vid/Shutterstock.

Contents

The suffixes -cious and -tious

The ending **–ious** can be added to turn nouns into adjectives. If the root word ends in **–ce**, the ending is **–cious**.

Remove the e before adding **–ious**: grace + ious = gra**cious**.

If the root word ends in **–tion**, the ending is **–tious**.

Remove the **–ion** before adding **–ious**: caution + ious = cau**tious**. There is one common exception: anx**ious**.

Get started

Sort these words into nouns and adjectives by looking at the word endings. Copy and complete the table. One has been done for you.

1. infectious

2. conscious

3. caution

4. infection

5. space

6. fictitious

7. cautious

8. spacious

9. grace

10. avarice

Nouns	Adjectives
	infectious

Try these

Choose the correct spelling of each word. One has been done for you.

1. spatious / spacious

   Answer: *spacious*

2. malicious / malitious

3. nutricious / nutritious

4. pretencious / pretentious

5. contencious / contentious

Copy and complete the sentences by choosing the correct spelling of each word. One has been done for you.

1. Sumo wrestlers must have _____ appetites. (voracious / voratious)

   Answer: *Sumo wrestlers must have voracious appetites.*

2. Liza never walks under ladders: she is _____.
   (supersticious / superstitious)

3. The greedy millionaire was an _____ man. (avaricious / avaritious)

4. My brother is always a _____ host. (gracious / gratious)

5. Be _____ when handling deadly snakes. (caucious / cautious)

Now try these

Change each noun to an adjective and use it in a sentence of your own. One has been done for you.

ambition, malice, nutrition, pretention, contention, vice, auspice, caprice, office, fraction

   Answer: *Seth's plan to sail around the world was ambitious.*

The suffixes -cial and -tial (1)

Some words end with the suffixes **-cial** and **-tial**. In these words, the letters **ci** and **ti** make a **/sh/** sound. These endings sound the same and we have to learn when to use **-cial** and when to use **-tial**. After a vowel, we usually use the ending **-cial**, for example: spe**cial**. After a consonant, we usually use the ending **-tial**, for example: torren**tial**.

Get started

Sort these words into two groups: words ending **-cial** and words ending **-tial**. Copy and complete the table. Underline the letter before the ending. Can you see a pattern? One has been done for you.

1. celestial

2. sequential

3. financial

4. presidential

5. racial

6. glacial

7. insubstantial

8. judicial

9. residential

10. preferential

Words ending -tial	Words ending -cial
cele<u>s</u>tial	

Try these

These words break the rule! Learn their spellings.

spatial

initial

palatial

commercial

provincial

Next, match each word to its root word and write the two words as a pair. One has been done for you.

spatial palatial space province commercial palace provincial commerce

Answer: space – spatial

Now try these

Copy and complete the sentences using the words from the box. One has been done for you.

financial influential celestial presidential sequential

1. Winning the lottery ended all Dan's _____ problems.

   Answer: Winning the lottery ended all Dan's financial problems.

2. A _____ body is an object in the sky, such as the Sun, the Moon or a planet.

3. The numbers 5, 6, 7 and 8 are _____.

4. The American _____ race is the competition for the next president.

5. The most _____ people in a young child's life are his or her parents.

The suffixes –cial and –tial (2)

Some words end with the suffixes **–cial** and **–tial**. In these words, the letters **ci** and **ti** stand for a **/sh/** sound. After a vowel, we usually use the ending **–cial**, for example: spe**cial**. After a consonant, we usually use the ending **–tial**, for example: torren**tial**.

Get started

Some of these words are spelt correctly; some are not. Create a table like the one below. Write the correctly spelt words in the left-hand column. One has been done for you. Correct those that need correcting and write them in the right-hand column.

1. artificial

2. quintessential

3. confidential

4. parcial

5. unoffitial

6. facial

7. potencial

8. superficial

9. beneficial

10. antisotial

Correct	Corrected
artificial	

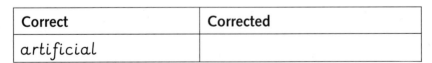

Try these

Add the correct suffixes to the following root words. Look carefully at the final letter of the root word before you make your decision. One has been done for you.

1. cru

2. poten

Answer: *crucial*

3. mar **4.** spe

5. benefi **6.** essen

7. substan **8.** par

Now try these

Copy the paragraphs and complete them by choosing the correct words. One has been done for you.

For Sandeep, it was <u>*crucial*</u> that he win this game of table tennis. A p_____l victory was not enough; he wanted the o_____ l title of champion. He had his s_____ l lucky bat in his hand. "Today has the p_____l to be a great day," said Sandeep.

Exercise is e_____ l to keeping fit. Training in m_____l arts could make a s_____l improvement to your fitness and may also be b_____l to your s_____l life.

The suffixes -ant or -ent

The endings **-ant** and **-ent** sound similar. Use **-ant** if there is a related word with the **/ay/** sound in the right position, for example: hesit**a**tion – hesit**ant**.

Use **-ent** after a soft **c**, after a soft **g** or if there is a related word with a clear **/e/** sound in the right position. For example: inno**c**ent, a**g**ent, confid**e**ntial – confid**ent**.

There are many words, however, that just have to be learned. For example: assist**ant**, obedi**ent** and independ**ent**.

Get started

Sort these words into two groups: words that end **-ent** and words that end **-ant**. One has been done for you. Colour the letters **c** and **g** in green where they stand for soft sounds and in blue where they stand for hard sounds. Can you see a pattern?

1. significant	**2.** magnificent	**3.** agent
4. vacant	**5.** detergent	**6.** elegant
7. indulgent	**8.** newsagent	**9.** arrogant
10. percent	**11.** applicant	**12.** recent
13. crescent	**14.** extravagant	**15.** descent

Words ending –ent	Words ending –ant
	significant

Try these

Copy and complete the table by adding the correct suffix to the root word. Say the related word out loud to get a clue for the ending.

Add –ent or –ant	Related word
hesitant	hesitation
confid	confidential
emerg	emergency
intellig	intelligently
applic	application
expect	expectation

Now try these

Write a sentence (as silly as you like) using each set of words. Use your sentences to help you remember the endings in future.

1. tyrant, insignificant, peasant, ant

Answer: *The tyrant thought the peasant was as insignificant as an ant.*

2. elegant, extravagant, arrogant, Anna

3. brilliant, elephant, triumphant, Anwar

4. prevent, accident, incident, bent

5. present, president, student, sent

The suffixes -ant, -ance/-ancy, -ent and -ence/-ency

The suffixes **–ance**, **–ancy**, **–ence** and **–ency** can be used to create a noun from an adjective, for example: eleg**ant** → eleg**ance**, urg**ent** → urg**ency**. If a related word ends **–ant**, use the suffix **–ance** or **–ancy**. If a related word ends **–ent**, use the suffix **–ence** or **–ency**.

These suffixes sound very similar and often the spelling just has to be learned.

Get started

Sort these words into two groups: words that end in **–ance/–ancy** and words that end in **–ence/–ency**. Copy and complete the table. One has been done for you.

1. infancy
2. residence
3. currency
4. occupancy
5. expectancy
6. fluency
7. emergence
8. observance

–ance / –ancy	–ence / –ency
infancy	

Try these

Copy and complete the table by adding the correct suffix to each root word to make the related adjectives and nouns. Listen to the final sound in the root word. One has been done for you.

Root	Adjective	Noun
neglig	*negligent*	*negligence*
magnific		
extravag		
eleg		
urg		
converg		

Now try these

Copy and complete the sentences by writing the correct spelling of each word. One has been done for you.

1. Mary was happy: at last she had her driving lic____.

   Answer: *Mary was happy: at last she had her driving licence.*

2. Ashley was confid_____ that she would pass the history test.

3. From the top of the mountain, there was a magnific_____ view.

4. The fire alarm rang with a sense of urg_____.

5. Chickens are not renowned for their intellig_____.

6. The soldier conducted himself with dec_____ and honour.

7. Though ineleg_____ on land, penguins are very eleg_____ under water.

8. There is evid_____ that monkeys are very intellig_____ animals.

Tricky common words (1)

Many common words have a consonant letter that is doubled. Generally, a consonant letter that is doubled means that the vowel sound before it is short. For example: emb**a**rrass, prof**e**ssion, **a**cc**o**mmodate. It's not a foolproof rule but it can help with remembering these spellings.

Get started

Write out these words and underline the short vowel and double letter that follows in each word. One has been done for you. Practise spelling each word three times.

1. suggest

   Answer: s<u>u</u>gg<u>e</u>st

2. embarrass

3. recommend

4. programme

5. profession

6. accommodate

7. accompany

8. according

9. opportunity

10. occupy

Try these

These words are missing their double letter. Write the words with the correct double letter. One has been done for you. Some words need two sets of double letters. Use long and short vowel sounds to help. But remember: not all short vowels need double consonants after them.

1. ocur   **2.** necesary   **3.** agresive   **4.** comitee

Answer: *occur*

5. comunicate   **6.** comunity   **7.** imediate   **8.** exagerate

Now try these

Copy and complete the sentences by choosing the correct spelling for each word. One has been done for you.

1. It quickly became _____ that the new boy, Samuel Rubb, was going to be trouble. (apparent / aparrent)

Answer: *It quickly became apparent that the new boy, Samuel Rubb, was going to be trouble.*

2. "I would _____ it if you could speak one at a time!" pleaded Mr Wright. (apreciate / appreciate)

3. Zak arrived home from school and _____ started playing on the computer. (imeddiately / immediately)

4. There was a note _____ to the door saying 'Enter at your own risk'. (attached / atacched)

5. "Please don't _____ me," said the lady. "I'm trying to count these rabbits." (interrupt / intterupt)

6. Fergus is an _____ violinist but he is too shy to join the school orchestra. (excellent / exccelent)

7. The number of people who turned up for the party did not _____ with the number invited. (coresppond / correspond)

The suffixes -able, -ible, -ably and -ibly

Some adjectives end with the suffixes **–able** or **–ible**. Their related adverbs end with the suffixes **–ably** or **–ibly**.

Usually, the **–able/–ably** ending is used if a complete root word can be heard before it. If there is no complete root word, then use **–ible/–ibly**. For example: **depend**able/**depend**ably, **poss**ible/**poss**ibly.

The **–able/–ably** endings are also used if there is a related word ending in **–ation**. For example: ador**able**/ador**ably**/ador**ation**.

If the root word ends in **y**, it usually becomes **i** before the suffix. For example: re**ly**/reli**able**. However, there are exceptions to this. For example: enjo**y**/enjo**yable**.

If the root word ends in **e**, the **e** is removed before adding **–able/–ably**. For example: admir**e**/admir**able**/admir**ably**. However, if the root word ends in **–ce** or **–ge**, then the **e** is **not** removed. For example: chang**e**/chang**eable**.

When the endings **–ible** and **–ibly** are added to words ending in **–e**, **–ce** or **–ge**, the **e** is removed. For example: forc**e**/forc**ible**/forc**ibly**.

Get started

Change each verb into an adverb by adding the correct suffix. One has been done for you.

1. adore

   Answer: *adorably*

2. comfort

3. accept

4. understand

5. notice

6. fashion

Try these

Change each verb into an adjective by adding the correct suffix. Look carefully at the verb endings. One has been done for you.

1. consider

Answer: *considerable*

2. collapse

3. vary

4. manage

5. response

6. imagine

7. sense

8. change

Now try these

Copy and complete the sentences by choosing the correct spelling for each word. One has been done for you.

1. 'This film was _____ the best this year,' typed Samir in his email. (arguably / argueably)

Answer: *'This film was arguably the best this year,' typed Samir in his email.*

2. Manuel is the most _____ bachelor in town. (eligeable / eligible)

3. The Mayor was persuaded by _____ protest. (forceible / forcible)

4. Many plastics are _____: they do not snap when bent. (pliable / plyable)

5. To Georgia, her old teddy bear was _____. (irreplacable / irreplaceable)

6. The advertisement for skydiving claimed the risks were _____. (negligeable / negligible)

7. A _____ boat is called a submarine. (submergeible / submergible)

8. Charlene's messy handwriting is _____. (illegeable / illegible)

9. The tension in the atmosphere was almost _____. (tangeible / tangible)

Review unit 1

Can you remember the spellings you've learned this term? Answer these questions to find out.

A. Can you turn these nouns into adjectives? Write the adjective.

1. grace
2. caution
3. space
4. ambition
5. elegance
6. comfort
7. notice

B. Choose the correct spelling. Write the correct word.

1. torrential / torrencial
2. palatial / palacial
3. delitious / delicious
4. spetial / special
5. initial / inicial
6. finantial / financial

C. Write the word missing from each sentence.

1. Caitlin knew she should be grateful for the op_____nity to learn to sail, but she wasn't.

2. "What should I do? What do you su_____st?" Jamila sobbed.

3. Hannah was emb_____d but proud when she received her certificate in assembly.

4. The children set up a co_____ee to organise the class fair.

5. It won't be ne_____ry to go early because Sasha is saving seats for us at the front.

D. Copy and complete the chart. Choose **a**, **e**, **–ence** or **–ance** to complete the words. One has been done for you.

negligent	neglig____
arrog_nt	arrog____
confid_nt	confid____
intellig_nt	intellig____
magnific_nt	magnific____
abs_nt	abs____

Adding suffixes beginning with vowels to words ending in –fer

When you add a suffix that starts with a vowel (for example **–ed** or **–ing**) to a word ending in **–fer**, the spelling rule depends on which syllable is stressed.

If the **second** syllable is stressed, double the **r** when adding the suffix.
If the second syllable is **not** stressed, do not double the **r.**

Get started

Add **–ed** to these words and decide if the **r** should be doubled or not. One has been done for you.

1. proffer

 Answer: *proffered*

2. buffer

3. pilfer

4. differ

5. defer

Listen to whether or not the **–fer** syllable is stressed after adding the suffix. Sort the words into two groups: words where **–fer** is stressed and words where it is not. Copy and complete the table.

–fer is stressed when the suffix is added	–fer is not stressed when the suffix is added

Try these

Add **–ing** and **–ence** to these words and decide if the **r** should be doubled or not. Copy and complete the table. One has been done for you.

Verb	Add –ing	Add –ence
confer	*conferring*	*conference*
transfer		
refer		
defer		
differ		
infer		

Now try these

Copy the paragraph and complete it by choosing the correct spelling for each word. One has been done for you.

When Adam saw Mr Whiskers in a tree, he _inferred_ that he was stuck and climbed up to rescue him. Unfortunately, Adam s_____d from a fear of heights, normally p_____g to stay on the ground. (In this, Adam and Mr Whiskers d_____d greatly – Mr Whiskers actually p_____d high places.) Adam was o_____d help by a firefighter who said: "What a pickle," r_____g to Adam's situation. After c_____g with Adam, the firefighter suggested t_____g Adam's weight from the tree to his shoulders. Adam was terrified but eventually d_____d to the firefighter's better judgement and was rescued.

Use of the hyphen after prefixes

Hyphens can be used to join a prefix to a root word, if adding it helps the reader with pronunciation or meaning. If the prefix ends in a vowel and the root word begins with a vowel, the hyphen tells the reader to say two separate syllables.

Get started

Insert the hyphen in each word to help with pronunciation. One has been done for you.

1. ultraangry

   Answer: *ultra-angry*

2. coown

3. antiageing

4. reeducate

5. reenter

6. deice

7. reelect

8. coordinate

9. cooperate

10. preelection

Try these

Choose the correct spelling for each word. One has been done for you.

1. pre-election / preelection

   Answer: *pre-election*

2. re-enter / reenter

3. re-accumulate / reaccumulate

4. non-sense / nonsense

5. re-educate / reeducate

6. anti-freeze / antifreeze

7. de-frost / defrost

8. co-educate / coeducate

9. co-ordinate / coordinate

10. re-bound / rebound

Now try these

Use each of your answers from 'Try these' in a sentence of your own. One has been done for you.

Answer: *The batsman hit the ball on the rebound.*

The /ee/ sound spelt ei after c

The rhyme '**i** before **e**, except after **c**' can help you to spell the **/ee/** sound. After **c**, the letters that make the **/ee/** sound are the other way around: **e** comes before **i**. There are a number of exceptions to the rule. These exceptions just need to be learned.

Get started

Sort these words into two groups: those that follow the rule '**i** before **e** except after **c**' and those that do not follow the rule. One has been done for you.

1. niece
2. protein
3. conceive
4. baddie
5. caffeine
6. neither
7. receive
8. either
9. seize
10. chief

Words that follow the rule	Words that do not follow the rule
niece	

Try these

Copy and complete the sentences by putting the jumbled letters in the correct order to spell the missing word. One has been done for you.

1. On Monday, I will visit my _____, Chloe. (eenci)

   Answer: *On Monday, I will visit my niece, Chloe.*

2. The _____ constable is a severe but reasonable man. (cfeih)

3. I am too trusting: I _____ everything I'm told. (elbeevi)

4. I challenge you to a duel, you lying, _____ scoundrel! (udeeflict)

5. Kitchens should always be clean and _____. (ihngeicy)

6. John lay on his bed and stared up at the _____. (nicegli)

7. The kitten was always causing _____. (ihsmfice)

8. The castle had been under _____ for many months. (igese)

9. On your birthday, it is usual to _____ gifts. (creeiev)

10. It was autumn and the corn had turned golden in the _____. (ledfis)

Now try these

Use each of the following words in a sentence of your own. One has been done for you.

relieved, mischievous, receipt, deceive, perceive, conceited, piece, achieve, retrieve, shriek

Answer: *After days apart, the cub was relieved to see his mother again.*

The letter string ough

The letter string **ough** is one of the trickiest spellings in English. It can be used to spell a number of different sounds.

For example: He had a nasty **cough**. (Here, **ough** rhymes with **off**.)

The baker threw the dough onto the table. (Here, **ough** rhymes with **no**.)

Get started

Find the misspelt words in each set – some have more than one. One has been done for you.

1. rough, ruff, ruph

   Answer: *ruph*

2. stough, stuff, stuph

3. coff, cow, cough

4. bough, bau, bow,

5. wow, wough, woe

6. thorough, corough, borough

7. doe, dow, dough,

8. through, threw, threu

9. trough, troff, troph

10. blue, blew, blough

Try these

There are ten misspelt words in this paragraph. Copy the paragraph and correct the spellings – they should all be spelt with **ough**. One has been done for you.

The harvest had been safely ~~brort~~ *brought* in by the people of the **burah**. "Perhaps I **ort** to **plow** the fields now," the farmer **thort** as she filled the cow's feeding **troff**. "Winter is coming and the weather is getting **ruff**." The old apple tree had already lost one of its **bows** in the autumn wind and, **althow** there had been a **drowt** all summer, now it looked like rain.

Now try these

Use each of the following words in a sentence of your own. One has been done for you.

brought, sought, thought, although, cough, trough, dough, rough, through, tough

Answer: *Paolo brought his new toy to school.*

Words with 'silent' letters

'Silent' letters are the letters you cannot detect from the way a word is pronounced. They exist because the pronunciation of many words in the English language has changed over time. Some letters are no longer pronounced, even though they still exist in the spellings.

Get started

Add letters to each of these words to correct the spellings. One has been done for you.

1. stomac

   Answer: stomach

2. sutle

3. rinkle

4. receit

5. condem

6. ryme

7. colum

8. nickers

9. bom

10. clim

Try these

Find the correctly spelt word(s) in each set – some have more than one. One has been done for you.

1. wayle, whale, wail

   Answer: *whale, wail*

2. plum, plumb, plumn

3. gnaw, nor, knaw

4. write, wriht, right

5. kneel, gneel, kneil

6. gnot, not, knot

7. knome, nohme, gnome

8. answer, ansher, arnser

9. island, aisland, iyland

10. limb, limp, limn

Now try these

Copy and complete the paragraph by finding 12 misspelt words and correcting the spellings. (They are all missing their 'silent' letters.) One has been done for you.

The ~~night~~ *knight* dismounted and unbuckled his **sord**. Exhausted, he rested a **wile** by an old **narled** oak tree and **restled** with his conscience. Night was approaching, his **nee** was wounded and his **stomac** was empty. He wanted to rest but, if he stopped, he might be too late to save the King, whom he had sworn a **solem** oath to protect. He clenched his **nuckles** and **nashed** his teeth with frustration. If only he **new wat** to do.

More words with 'silent' letters

Here are some more words with letters that no longer stand for a sound for you to learn.

Get started

Write out these words. Underline the letter that is 'silent'. One has been done for you.

1. ghost

   Answer: gh_ost

2. wrap

3. lamb

4. doubt

5. plumber

6. thumb

7. knitting

8. gnat

9. debt

10. knobbly

Try these

Copy and complete the sentences, choosing the right spelling. One has been done for you.

1. I was just _____ a note to Mum, when she walked in the door.
(writing / righting)

   Answer: I was just writing a note to Mum, when she walked in the door.

2. The last round in the quiz was 'General _____'.
(noledge / knowledge)

3. Cameron knew it was _____ to eat the last biscuit but he couldn't help himself. (ronge / wrong)

4. By the time I got home there was not one _____ of cake left.
(crumb / crumn)

5. There is a hockey match after school on _____.
(Wednsday / Wednesday)

6. Naomi sat on the back seat of the bus, _____ between a crying toddler and a snoring man. (sandwiched / sanwhiched)

7. Mum and Dad looked very _____ in their wedding photo.
(hansomn / handsome)

8. We regretted going past the 'Road Closed' _____ when we became stuck in a snow drift. (sign / sighn)

9. "Please be _____," said Dad. "Did you or did you not break the vase?" (honest / ohnest)

10. Mind your own _____. (business / buzzniss)

Now try these

Use each of the following words in a sentence of your own. Underline the letter that is 'silent'. One has been done for you.

salmon, autumn, column, ballet, listen, castle

   Answer: The bear stood by the river to catch the leaping salmon.

Tricky common words (2)

Many common words have tricky spellings. This is sometimes because the pronunciation of the word has changed over the years – although the spelling has not. One way to learn these words is to remember the part of the word that has a tricky spelling.

Get started

Write these words out three times. Underline the part of the word that is tricky. One has been done for you.

1. soldier

   Answer: sol<u>die</u>r sol<u>die</u>r sol<u>die</u>r

2. thorough

3. stomach

4. shoulder

5. secretary

6. restaurant

7. queue

8. privilege

Try these

Write down the correct spelling of each of these words. The first one has been done for you.

1. mischievous / mischifus

    Answer: *mischievous*

2. parliament / parliment

3. perswade / persuade

4. neighbour / neighber

5. marvellus / marvellous

6. nuisance / newsence

7. definit / definite

8. leisure / lesure

9. muscle / mussel

10. brooze / bruise

Now try these

Write a sentence for each of these words. Try to write a sentence that will help you to remember the spelling. One has been done for you.

yacht, disastrous, category, bargain, vegetable, vehicle

    Answer: *We sat on the deck of the yacht, watching the sunset and chatting.*

Can you remember the spellings you've learned this term? Answer these questions to find out.

A. Four of the words in this list are spelt incorrectly. Write out the list, correcting the spelling mistakes.

rough   feeld

transferring   referrence

receeve   through

weird   coff

B. Write the word by adding the prefix or suffix. Remember: you might need to change the spelling of the root word or use a hyphen. One has been done for you.

1. re– + enter =   **2.** prefer +– ed =

Answer: re-enter

3. buffer + –ed =   **4.** co– + own =

5. infer + –ing =   **6.** differ + –ence =

7. de + –ice =

C. Copy and complete each sentence, choosing the correct words to fill the gaps. One has been done for you.

1. Tomas was not impressed when his _____ Joseph arrived: Joseph had _____ his little sister with him. (frend / friend; brought / broght)

   Answer: *Tomas was not impressed when his friend Joseph arrived: Joseph had brought his little sister with him.*

2. Max had _____ top marks in all subjects but he was so _____ that nobody wanted to congratulate him.

   (achieved / acheeved; conceted / conceited)

3. Chatting to his _____ whilst mending the fence, Brian hit his _____ with the hammer. (neighbour / neighbour; thum / thumb)

D. The bold words in this paragraph are all spelt incorrectly. Write out the paragraph, correcting the spelling of each word.

Freya sat sobbing in her prison cell. **Nether** an escape nor a rescue seemed likely. She **thort** about her mother and longed to **rite** a letter to her. But there was no way she could **perswade** a guard to send a letter, let alone bring her an **anser**. Later, a new guard took up the post outside her room. He was young; possibly younger than Freya, and **defenetly** too young to be hard-hearted. Freya thought that, if she was **suttle**, she might be able to get him on her side and then, maybe, a letter – or even an escape – might be possible. She began to hope.

Tricky common words (3)

Many common words have unusual spellings that we need to learn. Many of them are straightforward to spell if we listen carefully to the sounds and don't panic!

Get started

Write out these words as two lists: words you can spell and words you need to practise. Write out the ones you need to practise three times. Underline the letters you need to remember.

1. sincerely
2. signature
3. awkward
4. twelfth
5. variety
6. physical
7. lightning
8. forty
9. amateur
10. foreign
11. frequently
12. government

Try these

Copy and complete each sentence, choosing the correct word to fill the gap. One has been done for you.

1. Poppy and Polly wanted to go to the Christmas pantomime but, unfortunately, there were no tickets _____.
   (available / avalable / availible)

   Answer: *Poppy and Polly wanted to go to the Christmas pantomime but, unfortunately, there were no tickets available.*

2. The one-way _____ around the city centre is always stationary at rush hour. (system / sistem / systim)

3. Athletes often _____ time with friends and family in order to train hard enough. (sacrefice / sacrifice / sacrifise)

4. It is crucial to know what sort of snake or spider has bitten a person so they can be given the _____ anti-venoms.
   (relevant / relavant / relevent)

5. Although English is spoken in many countries across the world, the _____ often varies.
   (pronounciation / pronunciation / pronuntiation)

6. An ampersand (&) is a _____ for the word 'and'.
   (simble / symble / symbol)

Now try these

Use each of the following words in a sentence of your own. One has been done for you.

hindrance, conscience, conscious, desperate, controversy, convenience

Answer: *Cinderella felt that her glass slippers were a terrible hindrance as she tried to run from the ball.*

Homophones and near-homophones (I)

Homophones are words that sound the same but are spelt differently and have different meanings. You always need context (a setting, for example, a sentence) to know which spelling to use. Often, the spellings of homophones just have to be learned.

Near-homophones are words that sound similar. They are also spelt differently and have different meanings.

Get started

Match each of these words to the correct synonym. One has been done for you.

desert, dessert, wary, weary, affect, effect, complement, compliment, precede, proceed

1. tired

   Answer: weary

2. progress

3. cautious

4. abandon

5. influence

6. pre-exist

7. consequence

8. pudding

9. addition

10. flatter

Try these

Copy and complete each sentence by choosing the correct word to fill in the gap. One has been done for you.

1. The teacher _____ David on his work. (complemented / complimented)

   Answer: *The teacher complimented David on his work.*

2. The parade _____ across the square to the Town Hall. (proceeded / preceded)

3. This terrible tragedy has _____ us all. (affected / effected)

4. Last night's storm _____ this morning's floods. (proceeded / preceded)

5. All _____ from the cake sale will go to charity. (proceeds / precedes)

6. At high noon, the sheriff found the streets _____. (desserted / deserted)

7. It was Marta's birthday so she had two _____ after her lunch! (desserts / deserts)

8. The man is infamous: his reputation _____ him. (proceeds / precedes)

Now try these

Write a sentence for each of these words. You can use prefixes and suffixes, but make sure the root is correct for the context. One has been done for you.

desert, dessert, wary, weary, affect, effect, complement, compliment, precede, proceed

   Answer: *Jana's blue hairband complements her eyes perfectly.*

Homophones and near-homophones (2)

Homophones are words that sound the same, but they are spelt differently and have different meanings. You always need context to know how to spell homophones. Some homophone pairs can be told apart because one of the words is a past-tense verb.

Get started

Match each word to the correct synonym. One has been done for you.

guessed, lead, past, guest, herd, led

1. estimated

   Answer: *guessed*

2. visitor

3. group

4. history

5. escorted

6. metal

In your own words, write a definition for each of these words. Use a dictionary if you need to. One has been done for you.

7. herd

   Answer: *herd: a group of animals*

8. passed

9. lead

10. heard

Try these

Copy and complete each sentence, choosing the correct word to fill the gap. One has been done for you.

1. Matilda _____ all the answers in her spelling test. (guest / guessed)

   Answer: *Matilda guessed all the answers in her spelling test.*

2. I can't dance: it's as though my feet are made of _____. (led / lead)

3. Fast asleep in baby bear's bed was an uninvited _____. (guest / guessed)

4. I've _____ it's very pleasant in Italy at this time of year. (herd / heard)

5. I _____ my swimming test with excellent marks! (past / passed)

6. The dog _____ the man to where the children were trapped. (led / lead)

7. The guide tried to _____ the tourists towards the exit. (herd / heard)

8. In the _____, wolves lived and thrived in Britain. (past / passed)

Now try these

Write a sentence for each of these words. One has been done for you.

guessed, guest, passed, past, led, lead, heard, herd (noun), herd (verb)

   Answer: *On the drive home, the family passed a river.*

Homophones and near-homophones (3)

Homophones are words that sound the same, but are spelt differently and have different meanings.

Some homophone pairs can be told apart because one of the words is a verb and the other is a noun. For example, **practice** (with a **c**) is a noun meaning 'a custom or procedure', such as in the sentence: 'Prayer is a practice observed by many religions'. **Practise** (with an **s**) is a verb and means: 'to repeat something in order to improve', as in the sentence: 'Carl practises the piano every day'.

Get started

Match a word to the correct synonym. There are two extra words. One has been done for you.

advice, license, advise, device, licence, prophecy, devise, practise, prophesy, practice

1. a permit

   Answer: *licence*

2. predict

3. invent

4. allow

5. suggest

6. carry out

7. recommendations

8. appliance

Try these

Decide whether each word is a verb or a noun and write a definition for each word. Use a dictionary if you need to. One has been done for you.

1. practice:

   Answer: *practice: noun, a custom or procedure*

2. advise:

3. prophecy:

4. licence:

5. prophesy:

6. devise:

7. practise:

8. license:

9. advice:

10. device:

Now try these

Write a sentence for each of these words. Use prefixes and suffixes if you want to but make sure the root is correct for the context. One has been done for you.

practice, practise, licence, license, prophecy, prophesy, advice, advise, device, devise

Answer: *Noah practised his singing until he had the voice of an angel.*

Homophones and near-homophones (4)

Homophones are words that sound the same, but are spelt differently and have different meanings. You always need context to know how to spell homophones. Often, the spellings of homophones just have to be learned.

Get started

Write a synonym for each of these words, using a dictionary if you need to. One has been done for you.

1. draft

　　Answer: *outline*

2. principal

3. aisle

4. principle

5. isle

6. serial

7. aloud

8. draught

9. allowed

10. stationary

11. cereal

12. stationery

Try these

Copy and complete each sentence, choosing the correct word to fill the gap. One has been done for you.

1. For breakfast, Kyle and his dad always ate _____. (cereal / serial)

   Answer: *For breakfast, Kyle and his dad always ate cereal.*

2. Children are not _____ near the water's edge. (aloud / allowed)

3. Envelopes are kept in the _____ cupboard. (stationary / stationery)

4. The _____ of Man is part of the United Kingdom. (Aisle / Isle)

5. The _____ of the school welcomed the new pupils. (principal / principle)

6. If you have a good idea, please speak your thoughts _____. (aloud / allowed)

7. The bride tripped on her dress as she walked down the _____. (aisle / isle)

8. Every Monday, Aleksy watched his favourite television _____. (cereal / serial)

9. Unmoving, unblinking, the tiger remained entirely _____. (stationary / stationery)

10. It is against my _____ to lie, cheat or swindle. (principals / principles)

Now try these

Write a sentence for each of these words. Use prefixes and suffixes if you want to but make sure the root is correct for the context. One has been done for you.

aisle, isle, serial, cereal, aloud, allowed, draft, draught, stationary, stationery

   Answer: *In this supermarket, cleaning products are found in aisle three.*

Homophones and near-homophones (5)

Homophones are words that sound the same, but are spelt differently and have different meanings. You always need context (a setting, for example, a sentence) to know how to spell homophones. Often, the spellings of homophones just have to be learned. For example, **bridle**: headgear for controlling a horse; **bridal**: of, or relating to, a bride.

Get started

Sort these words into their different word types – some of them fit into more than one category. Copy and complete the table, using a dictionary if you need to. One has been done for you.

1. ascent
2. bridle
3. descent
4. morning
5. father
6. bridal
7. mourning
8. profit
9. farther
10. prophet

Nouns	Verbs	Adjectives	Adverbs
mourning	*mourning*		

Try these

Write a definition for each of these words, using a dictionary if you need to. One has been done for you.

1. assent

   Answer: *assent: an agreement or to agree*

2. steel

3. morning

4. dissent

5. steal

6. mourning

7. ascent

8. whose

9. descent

10. who's

Now try these

Write a sentence for each of these words. Use prefixes and suffixes if you want to but make sure the root is correct for the context. One has been done for you.

whose, who's, ascent, assent, descent, dissent, father, farther, morning, mourning, steal, steel, bridal, bridle, profit, prophet

Answer: *"Whose smelly socks are these?" asked Mum.*

Review unit 3

Can you remember the spellings you've learned this term? Answer these questions to find out.

A. Match each word to the correct definition. Write the word and its definition. One has been done for you.

1. conscience   group of sheep or cows

2. conscious   praise

3. compliment   listened

4. complement   sense of right and wrong

5. herd   match well

6. heard   gave permission

7. aloud   awake and aware

8. allowed   for all to hear

Answer: *conscience: sense of right and wrong*

B. Copy and complete each sentence by choosing the correct word to fill in the gap. One has been done for you.

1. "It really isn't _____ whose fault it is; I just want the mess cleaned up now!" (relevant / relevent)

   Answer: *"It really isn't relevant whose fault it is; I just want the mess cleaned up now!"*

2. Mr and Mrs Smith loved going on luxurious _____ holidays. (foreihn / foreign)

3. The plot of the movie was very silly but the special _____ were excellent. (affects / effects)

4. We had just _____ the last service station when my sister said she needed the toilet. (passed / past)

5. At the back of the _____ cupboard, behind the pens and the paper, we found two squashed footballs, four Santa hats and an old orange. (stationary / stationery)

C. Read these sentences. The underlined word has been spelt incorrectly. Write out the sentence, correcting the spelling. One has been done for you.

1. A dove is a <u>cymbal</u> of peace.

   Answer: *A dove is a symbol of peace.*

2. We collected 50 <u>signitures</u> on our petition for healthier meals in the school canteen.

3. A bowl of <u>serial</u> can be a perfect late night snack.

4. Sitting in our leaking tent after a cold, muddy day, we were <u>desparate</u> to go home.

5. Picking Siva for the hockey team instead of Jamie caused <u>controvasy</u>.

6. I didn't understand the maths problem so I just <u>guest</u> the answer.

D. Use each of the following words in sentences of your own. One has been done for you.

1. advice

   Answer: *The best advice I've ever had was to learn a musical instrument.*

2. advise

3. practise

4. practice

5. father

6. farther